And *that* we know for sure!

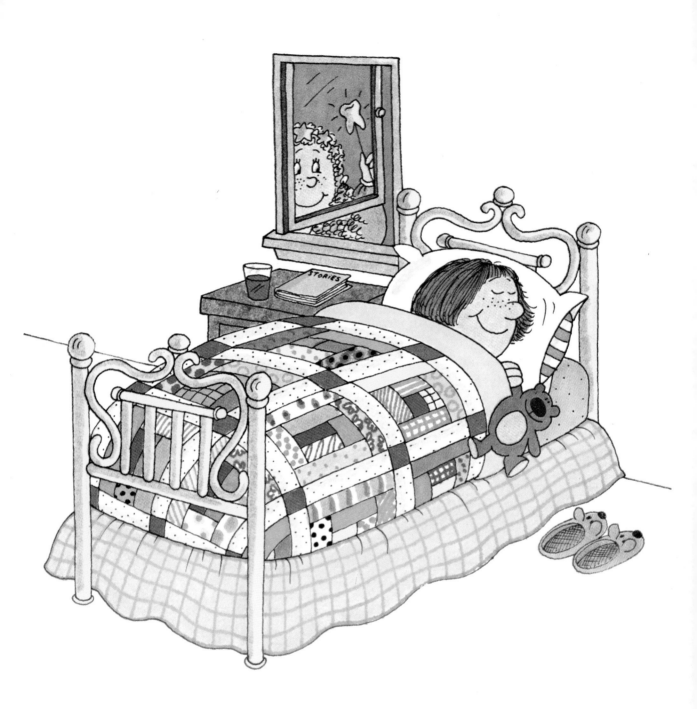

She comes and goes
when you are fast asleep.

And no one sees her go.

No one sees her come.

Sometimes she comes for two.

Sometimes she comes for one.

The Tooth Fairy comes when
you're fast asleep.

But one thing *is* for sure.

No one knows for sure.

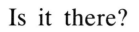

Is it there?

Is it here?

Where do all the teeth go?

No one knows for sure.

Is it late?

Is it early?

No one knows *when* the Tooth Fairy comes.

No one knows for sure.

Does she go by sea?

Does she go by air?

No one knows *how* the Tooth Fairy goes.

No one knows for sure.

Does she live in the South?

Does she live in the North?

No one knows for sure.

No one knows *where* the Tooth Fairy lives.

Library of Congress Cataloging in Publication Data

Peters, Sharon.
   The tooth fairy.

   Summary: Speculates on what is and is not
known about the Tooth Fairy.
   [1. Tooth Fairy—Fiction]   I. Sims, Deborah.
II. Title.
PZ7.P44183To   [E]   81-5100
ISBN 0-89375-519-2 (case)   AACR2
ISBN 0-89375-520-6 (pbk.)

The Tooth Fairy

Written by Sharon Peters

Illustrated by Deborah Sims

Troll Associates

A Giant First-Start Reader

This easy reader contains only 49 different words,
repeated often to help the young reader develop
word recognition and interest in reading.

Basic word list for *The Tooth Fairy*

air	goes	she
all	her	sometimes
and	here	South
are	how	sure
asleep	in	teeth
but	is	that
by	it	the
come	know	there
comes	knows	thing
do	late	tooth
does	live	two
early	lives	we
Fairy	no	when
fast	North	where
for	one	you
go	sea	you're
	sees	